VEHICLE & INSURAI

CW00408766

Vehicle Make/Model:

Plate Number:

Registration:

Contact Number:

Address:

Postal Code:

Insurance Company:

Policy Number:

Renewal Date Due:

INCOME

Month:_____   Week:_____

Day	Cash Job	Account Job	Commission	Tips	Mileage
Bal. Fwd					
Mon					
Tues					
Wed					
Thur					
Fri					
Sat					
Sun					
Total					

Other Income	
Total Balance	

Notes:

_____

_____

_____

_____

EXPENSES

Expenses	Total	Notes
Fuel		
Insurance & Road Tax		
Repairs & Services		
Cleaning		
Council Charges		
Taxi Base Rent & Care Hire		
Loan Repayments		
Parking		
Drawing (Own Wage)		
Cash/ Cheques Banked		
Others:		
Total Balance		

Total Income	
Total Expenses	
Cash In Hand C/F To Next Week	

Notes:

_____

_____

_____

_____

INCOME

Month:_____   Week:_____

Day	Cash Job	Account Job	Commission	Tips	Mileage
Bal. Fwd					
Mon					
Tues					
Wed					
Thur					
Fri					
Sat					
Sun					
Total					

Other Income	
Total Balance	

Notes:
_____

_____

_____

_____

EXPENSES

Expenses	Total	Notes
Fuel		
Insurance & Road Tax		
Repairs & Services		
Cleaning		
Council Charges		
Taxi Base Rent & Care Hire		
Loan Repayments		
Parking		
Drawing (Own Wage)		
Cash/ Cheques Banked		
Others:		
Total Balance		

Total Income	
Total Expenses	
Cash In Hand C/F To Next Week	

Notes:
_____
_____
_____
_____

INCOME

Month:_____   Week:_____

Day	Cash Job	Account Job	Commission	Tips	Mileage
Bal. Fwd					
Mon					
Tues					
Wed					
Thur					
Fri					
Sat					
Sun					
Total					

Other Income	
Total Balance	

Notes:
_____

_____

_____

_____

EXPENSES

Expenses	Total	Notes
Fuel		
Insurance & Road Tax		
Repairs & Services		
Cleaning		
Council Charges		
Taxi Base Rent & Care Hire		
Loan Repayments		
Parking		
Drawing (Own Wage)		
Cash/ Cheques Banked		
Others:		
Total Balance		

Total Income	
Total Expenses	
Cash In Hand C/F To Next Week	

Notes:

_____

_____

_____

_____

INCOME

Month:_____   Week:_____

Day	Cash Job	Account Job	Commission	Tips	Mileage
Bal. Fwd					
Mon					
Tues					
Wed					
Thur					
Fri					
Sat					
Sun					
Total					

Other Income	
Total Balance	

Notes:
_____
_____
_____
_____

EXPENSES

Expenses	Total	Notes
Fuel		
Insurance & Road Tax		
Repairs & Services		
Cleaning		
Council Charges		
Taxi Base Rent & Care Hire		
Loan Repayments		
Parking		
Drawing (Own Wage)		
Cash/ Cheques Banked		
Others:		
Total Balance		

Total Income	
Total Expenses	
Cash In Hand C/F To Next Week	

Notes:
_____
_____
_____
_____

INCOME

Month:_____   Week:_____

Day	Cash Job	Account Job	Commission	Tips	Mileage
Bal. Fwd					
Mon					
Tues					
Wed					
Thur					
Fri					
Sat					
Sun					
Total					

Other Income	
Total Balance	

Notes:
_____

_____

_____

_____

EXPENSES

Expenses	Total	Notes
Fuel		
Insurance & Road Tax		
Repairs & Services		
Cleaning		
Council Charges		
Taxi Base Rent & Care Hire		
Loan Repayments		
Parking		
Drawing (Own Wage)		
Cash/ Cheques Banked		
Others:		
Total Balance		

Total Income	
Total Expenses	
Cash In Hand C/F To Next Week	

Notes:

_____

_____

_____

_____

INCOME

Month:_____   Week:_____

Day	Cash Job	Account Job	Commission	Tips	Mileage
Bal. Fwd					
Mon					
Tues					
Wed					
Thur					
Fri					
Sat					
Sun					
Total					

Other Income	
Total Balance	

Notes:
_____

_____

_____

_____

EXPENSES

Expenses	Total	Notes
Fuel		
Insurance & Road Tax		
Repairs & Services		
Cleaning		
Council Charges		
Taxi Base Rent & Care Hire		
Loan Repayments		
Parking		
Drawing (Own Wage)		
Cash/ Cheques Banked		
Others:		
Total Balance		

Total Income	
Total Expenses	
Cash In Hand C/F To Next Week	

Notes:

_____

_____

_____

_____

INCOME   Month:_____   Week:_____

Day	Cash Job	Account Job	Commission	Tips	Mileage
Bal. Fwd					
Mon					
Tues					
Wed					
Thur					
Fri					
Sat					
Sun					
Total					

Other Income	
Total Balance	

Notes:
_____
_____
_____
_____

EXPENSES

Expenses	Total	Notes
Fuel		
Insurance & Road Tax		
Repairs & Services		
Cleaning		
Council Charges		
Taxi Base Rent & Care Hire		
Loan Repayments		
Parking		
Drawing (Own Wage)		
Cash/ Cheques Banked		
Others:		
Total Balance		

Total Income	
Total Expenses	
Cash In Hand C/F To Next Week	

Notes:

_____

_____

_____

_____

INCOME

Month:_____   Week:_____

Day	Cash Job	Account Job	Commission	Tips	Mileage
Bal. Fwd					
Mon					
Tues					
Wed					
Thur					
Fri					
Sat					
Sun					
Total					

Other Income	
Total Balance	

Notes:
_____

_____

_____

_____

EXPENSES

Expenses	Total	Notes
Fuel		
Insurance & Road Tax		
Repairs & Services		
Cleaning		
Council Charges		
Taxi Base Rent & Care Hire		
Loan Repayments		
Parking		
Drawing (Own Wage)		
Cash/ Cheques Banked		
Others:		
Total Balance		

Total Income	
Total Expenses	
Cash In Hand C/F To Next Week	

Notes:
_____
_____
_____
_____

INCOME

Month:_____   Week:_____

Day	Cash Job	Account Job	Commission	Tips	Mileage
Bal. Fwd					
Mon					
Tues					
Wed					
Thur					
Fri					
Sat					
Sun					
Total					

Other Income	
Total Balance	

Notes:
_____

_____

_____

_____

EXPENSES

Expenses	Total	Notes
Fuel		
Insurance & Road Tax		
Repairs & Services		
Cleaning		
Council Charges		
Taxi Base Rent & Care Hire		
Loan Repayments		
Parking		
Drawing (Own Wage)		
Cash/ Cheques Banked		
Others:		
Total Balance		

Total Income	
Total Expenses	
Cash In Hand C/F To Next Week	

Notes:
_____
_____
_____
_____

INCOME

Month:_____   Week:_____

Day	Cash Job	Account Job	Commission	Tips	Mileage
Bal. Fwd					
Mon					
Tues					
Wed					
Thur					
Fri					
Sat					
Sun					
Total					

Other Income	
Total Balance	

Notes:
_____
_____
_____
_____

EXPENSES

Expenses	Total	Notes
Fuel		
Insurance & Road Tax		
Repairs & Services		
Cleaning		
Council Charges		
Taxi Base Rent & Care Hire		
Loan Repayments		
Parking		
Drawing (Own Wage)		
Cash/ Cheques Banked		
Others:		
Total Balance		

Total Income	
Total Expenses	
Cash In Hand C/F To Next Week	

Notes:
_____

_____

_____

_____

INCOME

Month:_____   Week:_____

Day	Cash Job	Account Job	Commission	Tips	Mileage
Bal. Fwd					
Mon					
Tues					
Wed					
Thur					
Fri					
Sat					
Sun					
Total					

Other Income	
Total Balance	

Notes:
_____

_____

_____

_____

EXPENSES

Expenses	Total	Notes
Fuel		
Insurance & Road Tax		
Repairs & Services		
Cleaning		
Council Charges		
Taxi Base Rent & Care Hire		
Loan Repayments		
Parking		
Drawing (Own Wage)		
Cash/ Cheques Banked		
Others:		
Total Balance		

Total Income	
Total Expenses	
Cash In Hand C/F To Next Week	

Notes:
_____

_____

_____

_____

INCOME

Month:_____   Week:_____

Day	Cash Job	Account Job	Commission	Tips	Mileage
Bal. Fwd					
Mon					
Tues					
Wed					
Thur					
Fri					
Sat					
Sun					
Total					

Other Income	
Total Balance	

Notes:
_____

_____

_____

_____

EXPENSES

Expenses	Total	Notes
Fuel		
Insurance & Road Tax		
Repairs & Services		
Cleaning		
Council Charges		
Taxi Base Rent & Care Hire		
Loan Repayments		
Parking		
Drawing (Own Wage)		
Cash/ Cheques Banked		
Others:		
Total Balance		

Total Income	
Total Expenses	
Cash In Hand C/F To Next Week	

Notes:
_____
_____
_____
_____

INCOME   Month:_____   Week:_____

Day	Cash Job	Account Job	Commission	Tips	Mileage
Bal. Fwd					
Mon					
Tues					
Wed					
Thur					
Fri					
Sat					
Sun					
Total					

Other Income	
Total Balance	

Notes:
_____

_____

_____

_____

EXPENSES

Expenses	Total	Notes
Fuel		
Insurance & Road Tax		
Repairs & Services		
Cleaning		
Council Charges		
Taxi Base Rent & Care Hire		
Loan Repayments		
Parking		
Drawing (Own Wage)		
Cash/ Cheques Banked		
Others:		
Total Balance		

Total Income	
Total Expenses	
Cash In Hand C/F To Next Week	

Notes:

_____

_____

_____

_____

INCOME

Month:_____   Week:_____

Day	Cash Job	Account Job	Commission	Tips	Mileage
Bal. Fwd					
Mon					
Tues					
Wed					
Thur					
Fri					
Sat					
Sun					
Total					

Other Income	
Total Balance	

Notes:
_____

_____

_____

_____

EXPENSES

Expenses	Total	Notes
Fuel		
Insurance & Road Tax		
Repairs & Services		
Cleaning		
Council Charges		
Taxi Base Rent & Care Hire		
Loan Repayments		
Parking		
Drawing (Own Wage)		
Cash/ Cheques Banked		
Others:		
Total Balance		

Total Income	
Total Expenses	
Cash In Hand C/F To Next Week	

Notes:

_____

_____

_____

_____

INCOME

Month:_____   Week:_____

Day	Cash Job	Account Job	Commission	Tips	Mileage
Bal. Fwd					
Mon					
Tues					
Wed					
Thur					
Fri					
Sat					
Sun					
Total					

Other Income	
Total Balance	

Notes:
_____

_____

_____

_____

EXPENSES

Expenses	Total	Notes
Fuel		
Insurance & Road Tax		
Repairs & Services		
Cleaning		
Council Charges		
Taxi Base Rent & Care Hire		
Loan Repayments		
Parking		
Drawing (Own Wage)		
Cash/ Cheques Banked		
Others:		
Total Balance		

Total Income	
Total Expenses	
Cash In Hand C/F To Next Week	

Notes:

_____

_____

_____

_____

INCOME   Month:_____   Week:_____

Day	Cash Job	Account Job	Commission	Tips	Mileage
Bal. Fwd					
Mon					
Tues					
Wed					
Thur					
Fri					
Sat					
Sun					
Total					

Other Income	
Total Balance	

Notes:
_____

_____

_____

_____

EXPENSES

Expenses	Total	Notes
Fuel		
Insurance & Road Tax		
Repairs & Services		
Cleaning		
Council Charges		
Taxi Base Rent & Care Hire		
Loan Repayments		
Parking		
Drawing (Own Wage)		
Cash/ Cheques Banked		
Others:		
Total Balance		

Total Income	
Total Expenses	
Cash In Hand C/F To Next Week	

Notes:
_____
_____
_____
_____

INCOME

Month:_____   Week:_____

Day	Cash Job	Account Job	Commission	Tips	Mileage
Bal. Fwd					
Mon					
Tues					
Wed					
Thur					
Fri					
Sat					
Sun					
Total					

Other Income	
Total Balance	

Notes: _____

_____

_____

_____

EXPENSES

Expenses	Total	Notes
Fuel		
Insurance & Road Tax		
Repairs & Services		
Cleaning		
Council Charges		
Taxi Base Rent & Care Hire		
Loan Repayments		
Parking		
Drawing (Own Wage)		
Cash/ Cheques Banked		
Others:		
Total Balance		

Total Income	
Total Expenses	
Cash In Hand C/F To Next Week	

Notes:
_____
_____
_____
_____

INCOME

Month:_____   Week:_____

Day	Cash Job	Account Job	Commission	Tips	Mileage
Bal. Fwd					
Mon					
Tues					
Wed					
Thur					
Fri					
Sat					
Sun					
Total					

Other Income	
Total Balance	

Notes:
_____

_____

_____

_____

EXPENSES

Expenses	Total	Notes
Fuel		
Insurance & Road Tax		
Repairs & Services		
Cleaning		
Council Charges		
Taxi Base Rent & Care Hire		
Loan Repayments		
Parking		
Drawing (Own Wage)		
Cash/ Cheques Banked		
Others:		
Total Balance		

Total Income	
Total Expenses	
Cash In Hand C/F To Next Week	

Notes:

_____

_____

_____

_____

INCOME

Month:_____   Week:_____

Day	Cash Job	Account Job	Commission	Tips	Mileage
Bal. Fwd					
Mon					
Tues					
Wed					
Thur					
Fri					
Sat					
Sun					
Total					

Other Income	
Total Balance	

Notes:
_____
_____
_____
_____

EXPENSES

Expenses	Total	Notes
Fuel		
Insurance & Road Tax		
Repairs & Services		
Cleaning		
Council Charges		
Taxi Base Rent & Care Hire		
Loan Repayments		
Parking		
Drawing (Own Wage)		
Cash/ Cheques Banked		
Others:		
Total Balance		

Total Income	
Total Expenses	
Cash In Hand C/F To Next Week	

Notes:

_____

_____

_____

_____

INCOME

Month:_____ Week:_____

Day	Cash Job	Account Job	Commission	Tips	Mileage
Bal. Fwd					
Mon					
Tues					
Wed					
Thur					
Fri					
Sat					
Sun					
Total					

Other Income	
Total Balance	

Notes:
_____

_____

_____

_____

EXPENSES

Expenses	Total	Notes
Fuel		
Insurance & Road Tax		
Repairs & Services		
Cleaning		
Council Charges		
Taxi Base Rent & Care Hire		
Loan Repayments		
Parking		
Drawing (Own Wage)		
Cash/ Cheques Banked		
Others:		
Total Balance		

Total Income	
Total Expenses	
Cash In Hand C/F To Next Week	

Notes:

_____

_____

_____

_____

INCOME

Month:_____   Week:_____

Day	Cash Job	Account Job	Commission	Tips	Mileage
Bal. Fwd					
Mon					
Tues					
Wed					
Thur					
Fri					
Sat					
Sun					
Total					

Other Income	
Total Balance	

Notes:
_____

_____

_____

_____

EXPENSES

Expenses	Total	Notes
Fuel		
Insurance & Road Tax		
Repairs & Services		
Cleaning		
Council Charges		
Taxi Base Rent & Care Hire		
Loan Repayments		
Parking		
Drawing (Own Wage)		
Cash/ Cheques Banked		
Others:		
Total Balance		

Total Income	
Total Expenses	
Cash In Hand C/F To Next Week	

Notes:
_____
_____
_____
_____

INCOME

Month:_____   Week:_____

Day	Cash Job	Account Job	Commission	Tips	Mileage
Bal. Fwd					
Mon					
Tues					
Wed					
Thur					
Fri					
Sat					
Sun					
Total					

Other Income	
Total Balance	

Notes:

EXPENSES

Expenses	Total	Notes
Fuel		
Insurance & Road Tax		
Repairs & Services		
Cleaning		
Council Charges		
Taxi Base Rent & Care Hire		
Loan Repayments		
Parking		
Drawing (Own Wage)		
Cash/ Cheques Banked		
Others:		
Total Balance		

Total Income	
Total Expenses	
Cash In Hand C/F To Next Week	

Notes:

_____

_____

_____

_____

INCOME

Month:_____   Week:_____

Day	Cash Job	Account Job	Commission	Tips	Mileage
Bal. Fwd					
Mon					
Tues					
Wed					
Thur					
Fri					
Sat					
Sun					
Total					

Other Income	
Total Balance	

Notes:
_____

_____

_____

_____

EXPENSES

Expenses	Total	Notes
Fuel		
Insurance & Road Tax		
Repairs & Services		
Cleaning		
Council Charges		
Taxi Base Rent & Care Hire		
Loan Repayments		
Parking		
Drawing (Own Wage)		
Cash/ Cheques Banked		
Others:		
Total Balance		

Total Income	
Total Expenses	
Cash In Hand C/F To Next Week	

Notes:

_____

_____

_____

_____

INCOME

Month:_____   Week:_____

Day	Cash Job	Account Job	Commission	Tips	Mileage
Bal. Fwd					
Mon					
Tues					
Wed					
Thur					
Fri					
Sat					
Sun					
Total					

Other Income	
Total Balance	

Notes:

_____

_____

_____

_____

EXPENSES

Expenses	Total	Notes
Fuel		
Insurance & Road Tax		
Repairs & Services		
Cleaning		
Council Charges		
Taxi Base Rent & Care Hire		
Loan Repayments		
Parking		
Drawing (Own Wage)		
Cash/ Cheques Banked		
Others:		
Total Balance		

Total Income	
Total Expenses	
Cash In Hand C/F To Next Week	

Notes:
_____
_____
_____
_____

INCOME

Month:_____   Week:_____

Day	Cash Job	Account Job	Commission	Tips	Mileage
Bal. Fwd					
Mon					
Tues					
Wed					
Thur					
Fri					
Sat					
Sun					
Total					

Other Income	
Total Balance	

Notes:
_____

_____

_____

_____

EXPENSES

Expenses	Total	Notes
Fuel		
Insurance & Road Tax		
Repairs & Services		
Cleaning		
Council Charges		
Taxi Base Rent & Care Hire		
Loan Repayments		
Parking		
Drawing (Own Wage)		
Cash/ Cheques Banked		
Others:		
Total Balance		

Total Income	
Total Expenses	
Cash In Hand C/F To Next Week	

Notes:

_____

_____

_____

_____

INCOME

Month:_____   Week:_____

Day	Cash Job	Account Job	Commission	Tips	Mileage
Bal. Fwd					
Mon					
Tues					
Wed					
Thur					
Fri					
Sat					
Sun					
Total					

Other Income	
Total Balance	

Notes:
_____
_____
_____
_____

EXPENSES

Expenses	Total	Notes
Fuel		
Insurance & Road Tax		
Repairs & Services		
Cleaning		
Council Charges		
Taxi Base Rent & Care Hire		
Loan Repayments		
Parking		
Drawing (Own Wage)		
Cash/ Cheques Banked		
Others:		
Total Balance		

Total Income	
Total Expenses	
Cash In Hand C/F To Next Week	

Notes:

_____

_____

_____

_____

INCOME

Month:_____   Week:_____

Day	Cash Job	Account Job	Commission	Tips	Mileage
Bal. Fwd					
Mon					
Tues					
Wed					
Thur					
Fri					
Sat					
Sun					
Total					

Other Income	
Total Balance	

Notes:

_____

_____

_____

_____

EXPENSES

Expenses	Total	Notes
Fuel		
Insurance & Road Tax		
Repairs & Services		
Cleaning		
Council Charges		
Taxi Base Rent & Care Hire		
Loan Repayments		
Parking		
Drawing (Own Wage)		
Cash/ Cheques Banked		
Others:		
Total Balance		

Total Income	
Total Expenses	
Cash In Hand C/F To Next Week	

Notes:
_____
_____
_____
_____

INCOME

Month:_____   Week:_____

Day	Cash Job	Account Job	Commission	Tips	Mileage
Bal. Fwd					
Mon					
Tues					
Wed					
Thur					
Fri					
Sat					
Sun					
Total					

Other Income	
Total Balance	

Notes:
_____

_____

_____

_____

EXPENSES

Expenses	Total	Notes
Fuel		
Insurance & Road Tax		
Repairs & Services		
Cleaning		
Council Charges		
Taxi Base Rent & Care Hire		
Loan Repayments		
Parking		
Drawing (Own Wage)		
Cash/ Cheques Banked		
Others:		
Total Balance		

Total Income	
Total Expenses	
Cash In Hand C/F To Next Week	

Notes:
_____
_____
_____
_____

INCOME

Month:_____   Week:_____

Day	Cash Job	Account Job	Commission	Tips	Mileage
Bal. Fwd					
Mon					
Tues					
Wed					
Thur					
Fri					
Sat					
Sun					
Total					

Other Income	
Total Balance	

Notes:

_____

_____

_____

_____

EXPENSES

Expenses	Total	Notes
Fuel		
Insurance & Road Tax		
Repairs & Services		
Cleaning		
Council Charges		
Taxi Base Rent & Care Hire		
Loan Repayments		
Parking		
Drawing (Own Wage)		
Cash/ Cheques Banked		
Others:		
Total Balance		

Total Income	
Total Expenses	
Cash In Hand C/F To Next Week	

Notes:

_____

_____

_____

_____

INCOME

Month:_____   Week:_____

Day	Cash Job	Account Job	Commission	Tips	Mileage
Bal. Fwd					
Mon					
Tues					
Wed					
Thur					
Fri					
Sat					
Sun					
Total					

Other Income	
Total Balance	

Notes:

_____

_____

_____

_____

EXPENSES

Expenses	Total	Notes
Fuel		
Insurance & Road Tax		
Repairs & Services		
Cleaning		
Council Charges		
Taxi Base Rent & Care Hire		
Loan Repayments		
Parking		
Drawing (Own Wage)		
Cash/ Cheques Banked		
Others:		
Total Balance		

Total Income	
Total Expenses	
Cash In Hand C/F To Next Week	

Notes:
_____
_____
_____
_____

INCOME

Month:_____ Week:_____

Day	Cash Job	Account Job	Commission	Tips	Mileage
Bal. Fwd					
Mon					
Tues					
Wed					
Thur					
Fri					
Sat					
Sun					
Total					

Other Income	
Total Balance	

Notes:
_____
_____
_____
_____

EXPENSES

Expenses	Total	Notes
Fuel		
Insurance & Road Tax		
Repairs & Services		
Cleaning		
Council Charges		
Taxi Base Rent & Care Hire		
Loan Repayments		
Parking		
Drawing (Own Wage)		
Cash/ Cheques Banked		
Others:		
Total Balance		

Total Income	
Total Expenses	
Cash In Hand C/F To Next Week	

Notes:
_____

_____

_____

_____

INCOME

Month:_____   Week:_____

Day	Cash Job	Account Job	Commission	Tips	Mileage
Bal. Fwd					
Mon					
Tues					
Wed					
Thur					
Fri					
Sat					
Sun					
Total					

Other Income	
Total Balance	

Notes: _____

_____

_____

_____

EXPENSES

Expenses	Total	Notes
Fuel		
Insurance & Road Tax		
Repairs & Services		
Cleaning		
Council Charges		
Taxi Base Rent & Care Hire		
Loan Repayments		
Parking		
Drawing (Own Wage)		
Cash/ Cheques Banked		
Others:		
Total Balance		

Total Income	
Total Expenses	
Cash In Hand C/F To Next Week	

Notes:

_____

_____

_____

_____

INCOME

Month:_____   Week:_____

Day	Cash Job	Account Job	Commission	Tips	Mileage
Bal. Fwd					
Mon					
Tues					
Wed					
Thur					
Fri					
Sat					
Sun					
Total					

Other Income	
Total Balance	

Notes:
_____

_____

_____

_____

EXPENSES

Expenses	Total	Notes
Fuel		
Insurance & Road Tax		
Repairs & Services		
Cleaning		
Council Charges		
Taxi Base Rent & Care Hire		
Loan Repayments		
Parking		
Drawing (Own Wage)		
Cash/ Cheques Banked		
Others:		
Total Balance		

Total Income	
Total Expenses	
Cash In Hand C/F To Next Week	

Notes:

_____

_____

_____

_____

INCOME

Month:_____   Week:_____

Day	Cash Job	Account Job	Commission	Tips	Mileage
Bal. Fwd					
Mon					
Tues					
Wed					
Thur					
Fri					
Sat					
Sun					
Total					

Other Income	
Total Balance	

Notes:

_____

_____

_____

_____

EXPENSES

Expenses	Total	Notes
Fuel		
Insurance & Road Tax		
Repairs & Services		
Cleaning		
Council Charges		
Taxi Base Rent & Care Hire		
Loan Repayments		
Parking		
Drawing (Own Wage)		
Cash/ Cheques Banked		
Others:		
Total Balance		

Total Income	
Total Expenses	
Cash In Hand C/F To Next Week	

Notes:

_____

_____

_____

_____

INCOME

Month:_____   Week:_____

Day	Cash Job	Account Job	Commission	Tips	Mileage
Bal. Fwd					
Mon					
Tues					
Wed					
Thur					
Fri					
Sat					
Sun					
Total					

Other Income	
Total Balance	

Notes:

_____

_____

_____

_____

EXPENSES

Expenses	Total	Notes
Fuel		
Insurance & Road Tax		
Repairs & Services		
Cleaning		
Council Charges		
Taxi Base Rent & Care Hire		
Loan Repayments		
Parking		
Drawing (Own Wage)		
Cash/ Cheques Banked		
Others:		
Total Balance		

Total Income	
Total Expenses	
Cash In Hand C/F To Next Week	

Notes:

_____

_____

_____

_____

INCOME

Month:_____   Week:_____

Day	Cash Job	Account Job	Commission	Tips	Mileage
Bal. Fwd					
Mon					
Tues					
Wed					
Thur					
Fri					
Sat					
Sun					
Total					

Other Income	
Total Balance	

Notes:

_____

_____

_____

_____

EXPENSES

Expenses	Total	Notes
Fuel		
Insurance & Road Tax		
Repairs & Services		
Cleaning		
Council Charges		
Taxi Base Rent & Care Hire		
Loan Repayments		
Parking		
Drawing (Own Wage)		
Cash/ Cheques Banked		
Others:		
Total Balance		

Total Income	
Total Expenses	
Cash In Hand C/F To Next Week	

Notes:
_____
_____
_____
_____

INCOME

Month:_____   Week:_____

Day	Cash Job	Account Job	Commission	Tips	Mileage
Bal. Fwd					
Mon					
Tues					
Wed					
Thur					
Fri					
Sat					
Sun					
Total					

Other Income	
Total Balance	

Notes:
_____
_____
_____
_____

EXPENSES

Expenses	Total	Notes
Fuel		
Insurance & Road Tax		
Repairs & Services		
Cleaning		
Council Charges		
Taxi Base Rent & Care Hire		
Loan Repayments		
Parking		
Drawing (Own Wage)		
Cash/ Cheques Banked		
Others:		
Total Balance		

Total Income	
Total Expenses	
Cash In Hand C/F To Next Week	

Notes:
_____
_____
_____
_____

INCOME

Month:_____   Week:_____

Day	Cash Job	Account Job	Commission	Tips	Mileage
Bal. Fwd					
Mon					
Tues					
Wed					
Thur					
Fri					
Sat					
Sun					
Total					

Other Income	
Total Balance	

Notes:
_____

_____

_____

_____

EXPENSES

Expenses	Total	Notes
Fuel		
Insurance & Road Tax		
Repairs & Services		
Cleaning		
Council Charges		
Taxi Base Rent & Care Hire		
Loan Repayments		
Parking		
Drawing (Own Wage)		
Cash/ Cheques Banked		
Others:		
Total Balance		

Total Income	
Total Expenses	
Cash In Hand C/F To Next Week	

Notes:
_____
_____
_____
_____

INCOME

Month:_____   Week:_____

Day	Cash Job	Account Job	Commission	Tips	Mileage
Bal. Fwd					
Mon					
Tues					
Wed					
Thur					
Fri					
Sat					
Sun					
Total					

Other Income	
Total Balance	

Notes:
_____

_____

_____

_____

EXPENSES

Expenses	Total	Notes
Fuel		
Insurance & Road Tax		
Repairs & Services		
Cleaning		
Council Charges		
Taxi Base Rent & Care Hire		
Loan Repayments		
Parking		
Drawing (Own Wage)		
Cash/ Cheques Banked		
Others:		
Total Balance		

Total Income	
Total Expenses	
Cash In Hand C/F To Next Week	

Notes:

_____

_____

_____

_____

INCOME

Month:_____   Week:_____

Day	Cash Job	Account Job	Commission	Tips	Mileage
Bal. Fwd					
Mon					
Tues					
Wed					
Thur					
Fri					
Sat					
Sun					
Total					

Other Income	
Total Balance	

Notes:
_____
_____
_____
_____

EXPENSES

Expenses	Total	Notes
Fuel		
Insurance & Road Tax		
Repairs & Services		
Cleaning		
Council Charges		
Taxi Base Rent & Care Hire		
Loan Repayments		
Parking		
Drawing (Own Wage)		
Cash/ Cheques Banked		
Others:		
Total Balance		

Total Income	
Total Expenses	
Cash In Hand C/F To Next Week	

Notes:
_____

_____

_____

_____

INCOME

Month:_____   Week:_____

Day	Cash Job	Account Job	Commission	Tips	Mileage
Bal. Fwd					
Mon					
Tues					
Wed					
Thur					
Fri					
Sat					
Sun					
Total					

Other Income	
Total Balance	

Notes:
_____

_____

_____

_____

EXPENSES

Expenses	Total	Notes
Fuel		
Insurance & Road Tax		
Repairs & Services		
Cleaning		
Council Charges		
Taxi Base Rent & Care Hire		
Loan Repayments		
Parking		
Drawing (Own Wage)		
Cash/ Cheques Banked		
Others:		
Total Balance		

Total Income	
Total Expenses	
Cash In Hand C/F To Next Week	

Notes:
_____
_____
_____
_____

INCOME

Month:_____   Week:_____

Day	Cash Job	Account Job	Commission	Tips	Mileage
Bal. Fwd					
Mon					
Tues					
Wed					
Thur					
Fri					
Sat					
Sun					
Total					

Other Income	
Total Balance	

Notes:

_____

_____

_____

_____

EXPENSES

Expenses	Total	Notes
Fuel		
Insurance & Road Tax		
Repairs & Services		
Cleaning		
Council Charges		
Taxi Base Rent & Care Hire		
Loan Repayments		
Parking		
Drawing (Own Wage)		
Cash/ Cheques Banked		
Others:		
Total Balance		

Total Income	
Total Expenses	
Cash In Hand C/F To Next Week	

Notes:
_____
_____
_____
_____

INCOME

Month:_____   Week:_____

Day	Cash Job	Account Job	Commission	Tips	Mileage
Bal. Fwd					
Mon					
Tues					
Wed					
Thur					
Fri					
Sat					
Sun					
Total					

Other Income	
Total Balance	

Notes:
_____

_____

_____

_____

EXPENSES

Expenses	Total	Notes
Fuel		
Insurance & Road Tax		
Repairs & Services		
Cleaning		
Council Charges		
Taxi Base Rent & Care Hire		
Loan Repayments		
Parking		
Drawing (Own Wage)		
Cash/ Cheques Banked		
Others:		
Total Balance		

Total Income	
Total Expenses	
Cash In Hand C/F To Next Week	

Notes:
_____
_____
_____
_____

INCOME

Month:_____   Week:_____

Day	Cash Job	Account Job	Commission	Tips	Mileage
Bal. Fwd					
Mon					
Tues					
Wed					
Thur					
Fri					
Sat					
Sun					
Total					

Other Income	
Total Balance	

Notes:
_____

_____

_____

_____

EXPENSES

Expenses	Total	Notes
Fuel		
Insurance & Road Tax		
Repairs & Services		
Cleaning		
Council Charges		
Taxi Base Rent & Care Hire		
Loan Repayments		
Parking		
Drawing (Own Wage)		
Cash/ Cheques Banked		
Others:		
Total Balance		

Total Income	
Total Expenses	
Cash In Hand C/F To Next Week	

Notes:

_____

_____

_____

_____

INCOME

Month:_____   Week:_____

Day	Cash Job	Account Job	Commission	Tips	Mileage
Bal. Fwd					
Mon					
Tues					
Wed					
Thur					
Fri					
Sat					
Sun					
Total					

Other Income	
Total Balance	

Notes:

_____

_____

_____

_____

EXPENSES

Expenses	Total	Notes
Fuel		
Insurance & Road Tax		
Repairs & Services		
Cleaning		
Council Charges		
Taxi Base Rent & Care Hire		
Loan Repayments		
Parking		
Drawing (Own Wage)		
Cash/ Cheques Banked		
Others:		
Total Balance		

Total Income	
Total Expenses	
Cash In Hand C/F To Next Week	

Notes:

_____

_____

_____

_____

INCOME

Month:_____   Week:_____

Day	Cash Job	Account Job	Commission	Tips	Mileage
Bal. Fwd					
Mon					
Tues					
Wed					
Thur					
Fri					
Sat					
Sun					
Total					

Other Income	
Total Balance	

Notes:
_____
_____
_____
_____

EXPENSES

Expenses	Total	Notes
Fuel		
Insurance & Road Tax		
Repairs & Services		
Cleaning		
Council Charges		
Taxi Base Rent & Care Hire		
Loan Repayments		
Parking		
Drawing (Own Wage)		
Cash/ Cheques Banked		
Others:		
Total Balance		

Total Income	
Total Expenses	
Cash In Hand C/F To Next Week	

Notes:

_____

_____

_____

_____

INCOME

Month:_____   Week:_____

Day	Cash Job	Account Job	Commission	Tips	Mileage
Bal. Fwd					
Mon					
Tues					
Wed					
Thur					
Fri					
Sat					
Sun					
Total					

Other Income	
Total Balance	

Notes:
_____
_____
_____
_____

EXPENSES

Expenses	Total	Notes
Fuel		
Insurance & Road Tax		
Repairs & Services		
Cleaning		
Council Charges		
Taxi Base Rent & Care Hire		
Loan Repayments		
Parking		
Drawing (Own Wage)		
Cash/ Cheques Banked		
Others:		
Total Balance		

Total Income	
Total Expenses	
Cash In Hand C/F To Next Week	

Notes:

_____

_____

_____

_____

INCOME

Month:_____   Week:_____

Day	Cash Job	Account Job	Commission	Tips	Mileage
Bal. Fwd					
Mon					
Tues					
Wed					
Thur					
Fri					
Sat					
Sun					
Total					

Other Income	
Total Balance	

Notes:

_____

_____

_____

_____

EXPENSES

Expenses	Total	Notes
Fuel		
Insurance & Road Tax		
Repairs & Services		
Cleaning		
Council Charges		
Taxi Base Rent & Care Hire		
Loan Repayments		
Parking		
Drawing (Own Wage)		
Cash/ Cheques Banked		
Others:		
Total Balance		

Total Income	
Total Expenses	
Cash In Hand C/F To Next Week	

Notes:

_____

_____

_____

_____

INCOME

Month:_____   Week:_____

Day	Cash Job	Account Job	Commission	Tips	Mileage
Bal. Fwd					
Mon					
Tues					
Wed					
Thur					
Fri					
Sat					
Sun					
Total					

Other Income	
Total Balance	

Notes:

_____

_____

_____

_____

EXPENSES

Expenses	Total	Notes
Fuel		
Insurance & Road Tax		
Repairs & Services		
Cleaning		
Council Charges		
Taxi Base Rent & Care Hire		
Loan Repayments		
Parking		
Drawing (Own Wage)		
Cash/ Cheques Banked		
Others:		
Total Balance		

Total Income	
Total Expenses	
Cash In Hand C/F To Next Week	

Notes:

_____

_____

_____

_____

INCOME

Month:_____   Week:_____

Day	Cash Job	Account Job	Commission	Tips	Mileage
Bal. Fwd					
Mon					
Tues					
Wed					
Thur					
Fri					
Sat					
Sun					
Total					

Other Income	
Total Balance	

Notes:
_____
_____
_____
_____

EXPENSES

Expenses	Total	Notes
Fuel		
Insurance & Road Tax		
Repairs & Services		
Cleaning		
Council Charges		
Taxi Base Rent & Care Hire		
Loan Repayments		
Parking		
Drawing (Own Wage)		
Cash/ Cheques Banked		
Others:		
Total Balance		

Total Income	
Total Expenses	
Cash In Hand C/F To Next Week	

Notes:
_____
_____
_____
_____

INCOME

Month:_____   Week:_____

Day	Cash Job	Account Job	Commission	Tips	Mileage
Bal. Fwd					
Mon					
Tues					
Wed					
Thur					
Fri					
Sat					
Sun					
Total					

Other Income	
Total Balance	

Notes:
_____
_____
_____
_____

EXPENSES

Expenses	Total	Notes
Fuel		
Insurance & Road Tax		
Repairs & Services		
Cleaning		
Council Charges		
Taxi Base Rent & Care Hire		
Loan Repayments		
Parking		
Drawing (Own Wage)		
Cash/ Cheques Banked		
Others:		
Total Balance		

Total Income	
Total Expenses	
Cash In Hand C/F To Next Week	

Notes:
_____
_____
_____
_____

INCOME

Month:_____   Week:_____

Day	Cash Job	Account Job	Commission	Tips	Mileage
Bal. Fwd					
Mon					
Tues					
Wed					
Thur					
Fri					
Sat					
Sun					
Total					

Other Income	
Total Balance	

Notes: _____

_____

_____

_____

EXPENSES

Expenses	Total	Notes
Fuel		
Insurance & Road Tax		
Repairs & Services		
Cleaning		
Council Charges		
Taxi Base Rent & Care Hire		
Loan Repayments		
Parking		
Drawing (Own Wage)		
Cash/ Cheques Banked		
Others:		
Total Balance		

Total Income	
Total Expenses	
Cash In Hand C/F To Next Week	

Notes:

_____

_____

_____

_____

INCOME

Month:_____ Week:_____

Day	Cash Job	Account Job	Commission	Tips	Mileage
Bal. Fwd					
Mon					
Tues					
Wed					
Thur					
Fri					
Sat					
Sun					
Total					

Other Income	
Total Balance	

Notes:
_____

_____

_____

_____

EXPENSES

Expenses	Total	Notes
Fuel		
Insurance & Road Tax		
Repairs & Services		
Cleaning		
Council Charges		
Taxi Base Rent & Care Hire		
Loan Repayments		
Parking		
Drawing (Own Wage)		
Cash/ Cheques Banked		
Others:		
Total Balance		

Total Income	
Total Expenses	
Cash In Hand C/F To Next Week	

Notes:

_____

_____

_____

_____

Thank you so much for choosing to purchase our book. We hope you enjoy it! If you do, we kindly request you to write a review on Amazon. It will help us maintain high-quality products while also supporting potential buyers in making informed decisions.

Want free goodies?
Email us: Blackforestpublications@gmail.com

@ Black Forest Publications

BLACK_FOREST_PUBLICATIONS

1. Open app
2. Go to bar
3. Tap to scan

Copyright© 2022 By Black Forest Publications